EGYPT

Gina Cline   Joi Washington

Farms need the river.

Plants need the river.

Trees need the river.

Camels need the river.

Goats need the river.

Cows need the river.

Men need the river.

Women need the river.

Boats need the river.

Stores need the river.

Factories need the river.

Cities need the river.

Egypt

Africa

Mediterranean Sea

Egypt

Red Sea

Atlantic Ocean

Indian Ocean

14

The World

POWER WORD

the